Let's Not Forget God

Let's Not Forget God

Freedom of Faith, Culture, and Politics

CARDINAL ANGELO SCOLA

Translated by Matthew Sherry

IMAGE
NEW YORK

IMAGE is a registered trademark and the "I" colophon
is a trademark of Random House LLC.

Originally published in Italy as *Non dementichiamoci di Dio: liberte di fedi
di culture e politice* by RCS Libri S.p.A., Milano, in 2013.
Copyright © 2013 by RCS Libri S.p.A., Milano.

Library of Congress Cataloging-in-Publication data is available upon request.

ISBN 978-0-8041-3899-4
eBook ISBN 978-0-8041-3900-7

Printed in the United States of America

Book design by Jennifer Daddio / Bookmark Design & Media Inc.
Cover design by Deanna DeStefano

1 3 5 7 9 10 8 6 4 2

First Edition

Contents

Foreword

JOHN L. ALLEN JR.

If real life resembled an episode of the American television series *Fringe*, there would be a device through which one could peer into the alternate universe where Cardinal Angelo Scola of Milan, for decades one of the most widely respected figures at the senior level of the Catholic Church, is the pope.

The show's premise is that there's a parallel reality next to this one where the same people inhabit the same space, but they play different roles based on plausible alternative trajectories their lives have taken. Certainly the papacy is such a credible arc for the seventy-two-year-old Scola, who in the eyes of virtually everyone who tracks Church affairs has the right stuff to lead. That's why he was at the top of most handicapping sheets heading into the conclave of 2013, which gathered in Rome to elect a successor to Pope Benedict XVI.

Of course, things in this universe turned out differently. The conclave turned instead to Cardinal Jorge Mario Bergoglio of Buenos Aires, Argentina, who took the name of Francis and who ever since has taken the world by storm. Yet that outcome did not change the fact that Scola continues to be among the most interesting and influential churchmen on the global stage.

I can testify from personal experience that journalistic exchanges with Scola are a gripping affair. He's capable of offering homespun pastoral wisdom in one breath and lofty intellectual formulas in the next, and he's not the kind of interview one ever dares to enter unprepared. He's uninhibited with reporters, which usually points to someone who's thought deeply about things and isn't skittish about his capacity to back up his convictions.

What this short book offers, therefore, is insight into how a true Catholic heavyweight approaches the Church's most consequential political concern today, which is religious freedom. One may dissent from the premises and conclusions Scola presents, but if one wishes to understand Catholicism, especially how it thinks about the intersection of faith and political life, this book is indispensable.

The text presents an extended version of the "Discourse to the City" Scola delivered on December 6, 2012. The cardinal archbishop of Milan traditionally delivers a lecture on the city's patronal feast of Saint Ambrose, and given the caliber of the men who've held the position in recent decades—acclaimed Cardinals Carlo Maria Martini and Dionigi Tettamanzi, and now Scola himself, all at one time considered contenders for the papacy—the speech is always a major civic and media event.

On this occasion Scola organized his remarks around the 1,700th anniversary of the Edict of Milan, the famous ruling by Emperors Constantine and Licinius in 313 AD halting the persecution of Christianity within ancient Roman territories. Scola styled it as the birth of religious freedom in the West. He also offered a warning about currents within contemporary society that are styled as religious "neutrality" but that, in his eyes, amount to the imposition of a secularist worldview at the expense of religious conceptions of life.

As Scola notes, the speech aroused intense reactions.

Vito Mancuso, a well-known progressive theologian and editorialist in Italy, published an essay in *La Repubblica* arguing that the Edict of Milan actually signaled the beginning of state sponsorship of Christianity at the expense of other religions, suggesting that Scola seemed nostalgic for a bygone era in which the state was subordinate to the Church.

Paolo Naso, an academic and member of the Federation of Evangelical Churches in Italy, accused Scola of launching a new "Cold War" against secularism, contrasting the speech negatively with the open and dialogic tone he associated with Martini and Tettamanzi. That reading was exacerbated by ominous newspaper headlines suggesting that Scola had dared to criticize the "lay state," understood in Italy to refer to the hard-won emancipation of civil society from clerical domination.

Such objections are probably part of what Scola has in mind when he wryly notes that "speaking about religious freedom today is rather arduous." He replies to his critics indirectly in this expanded version of his lecture, insisting that he is not talking about rolling back the clock; as he puts it, "There is no room in my thought for any return to the past."

Nevertheless, he insists that implicit within the

Edict of Milan, whatever its subsequent historical development, was a vision of religious liberty for all, rooted in the conviction that religion is a positive force for the commonweal. That's as opposed to the contemporary European conception of religious freedom as a way of restraining what secularists see as the essentially negative impact of religious passions on social cohesion.

In Scola's eyes, religious freedom should imply freedom for religion, as opposed to later formulations dating from the French Revolution that treat it as freedom from religion. What he seeks, he writes, is a social environment in which "free religious subjects" are encouraged to bring their "substantive ethics" into debates, though without imposing them on anyone. In so doing, Scola believes society can avoid two chronic temptations: that of the state using religion as an *instrumentum regni*, a tool of governing, and that of the church using the state as an *instrumentum salvationis*, a tool for bringing people to salvation.

The core of his case is that religious freedom is the "emblematic expression of freedom of conscience," and if it is not placed firmly "at the head of the scale of fundamental rights," then the entire edifice "is destined to crumble."

One fascinating insight Scola offers along the way is that for the ancient, it was religion itself that was "free," while for the modern it's the individual who must be free in religious matters. The challenge for postmodern secular society is how to articulate a positive vision of religious freedom, and the public role of religion, from within this personalist framework. Especially interesting in that regard are his thoughts on conscientious objection at the end of the text, an argument that ought to be especially compelling within the subjective philosophical framework of most Western conversation.

In the project of elaborating a new vision of religious freedom, Americans will be interested to know, Scola believes our legal and philosophical tradition is better positioned to lead the way than Europe's.

However one parses his argument, it's beyond dispute that religious freedom is destined to be the premier Catholic social and political concern of this era. That's because of not only mounting church/state tensions in the West but also the far more dramatic situation in other parts of the world, where a highly literal war on religion is being waged, often with Christians as its primary victims. The early twenty-first century is witnessing the rise of a new generation of Christian martyrs in regions such as the Middle East, sub-Saharan Africa, and parts of Asia, and defending both the rights and the very lives of those believers is bound to occupy a growing share of the Church's time and energy.

We may not have a contraption that allows us to see parallel universes, but all one needs is clear-eyed vision in this one to recognize that the present book offers one of Catholicism's premier thinkers and leaders wrestling with a burning social question. For anyone concerned with religion and the common good, *Let's Not Forget God* by Cardinal Angelo Scola is a must-read.

John L. Allen Jr. is senior correspondent for the National Catholic Reporter, *senior Vatican analyst for CNN, and author of* The Global War on Christians: Dispatches from the Front Lines of Anti-Christian Persecution *(Image Books).*

Preface

This book came about through the preparation of the speech that for many years the archbishop of Milan has addressed to the city on the occasion of the feast of Saint Ambrose. The idea of this annual speech dates back to the deceased cardinal archbishop of Milan Blessed Ildefonso Schuster, but it began to take on greater importance with Cardinal Giovanni Battista Montini (archbishop of Milan and later Pope Paul VI) and in a particular way with Cardinal Giovanni Colombo. Why a speech from the bishop of Milan on this occasion? The reason is clear. Saint Ambrose is the city's patron. Before being elected bishop of Milan he was a statesman, and he maintained this sensibility as a bishop, while obviously reshaping it to fit his new responsibilities as pastor. On the occasion of his feast and in light of his legacy, the bishop of

Milan offers to all citizens a few reflections of a general nature on aspects of public life. The theme for my presentation in the Basilica of Saint Ambrose during vespers on December 6, 2012, was, in a certain sense, compulsory. This year marks the celebration of the 1,700-year anniversary of the Edict of Milan. However one may wish to interpret the edict, it is beyond doubt that 2013 provides a special opportunity for exploring the topic of religious freedom. Its relevance is plain. Just as evident is its complexity.

After I began to prepare this text during the summer, it seemed to take on a life of its own and grew well beyond the limitations of the presentation, in which I faced the necessity of concentrating into half an hour the many aspects of the question and had to make many substantial deletions.

The Saint Ambrose speech has become a launching point for a lively debate (still under way today as I write these lines). From this has emerged the book that the reader now holds in his hands.

In making adjustments to the original manuscript, I have tried to take into account the many responses to the Saint Ambrose speech, although a lack of time, among other factors, has prevented me from examining them in detail one by one. I must say that all of them have been helpful. Out of respect for the reader, it seems that I must state my general opinion in this regard.

The comments have been essentially of three kinds. Some have sought to explore or to clarify the more problematic elements of the speech. Others, in spite of their painstaking composition, have not succeeded in avoiding certain prejudices. Proof of this may be found in the fact that in order to criticize the text, sometimes harshly, they have had to introduce categories that I did not use. I do not intend to deny the usefulness or seriousness of the work of these commentators, even if in some cases it is clear that they have not read the whole speech. The third type of comment is marked by strong prejudice, sometimes vented in insults, supported by no arguments other than those borrowed too rapidly from the two previous kinds of responses. Nonetheless I am thankful to all, if only because they have seen fit to consider my speech. And this is precisely the aim of the speech from the archbishop to the city on the occasion of the feast of Saint Ambrose.

The reader now has the opportunity to see first-hand what my convictions may be in these matters. Obviously mine is intended to be the contribution of a pastor of the Church who takes on problems that are particularly widely debated today. These have a considerable impact on the expression of the religions and cultural visions, including agnosticism and atheism, that inhabit the pluralist democracies of the West.

I will permit myself to make just two side notes on the contents of this book. Contrary to what many have written, there is no room in my reflection for any return to the past. This—and here I make my second side note—can clearly be gathered from my two previous works: *Una nuova laicità. Temi per una società plurale* (A new secularism: Ideas for a pluralist society) (Venice: Marsilio, 2007) and *Buone ragioni per la vita in comune. Religione, politica, economia* (Good reasons for life in common: Religion, politics, economy) (Milan: Mondadori, 2010). The present book is situated in continuity with these two writings.

To an objective reader, this text will seem to be aimed more at bringing up problems than at providing prefabricated solutions.

The question of religious freedom, closely connected to that of freedom of conscience, is revealing itself today to be crucial not only to the development of Western societies but also to the peaceful evolution of their relationships with Asia, Africa, and Latin America.

> *Cardinal Angelo Scola*
> *Archbishop of Milan*
> *Milan, January 6, 2013*
> *Solemnity of the Epiphany of the Lord*

Let's Not Forget God

I

An Opportunity for Reflection

The seventeenth centenary of the Edict of Milan brings back to our attention the issue, more relevant than ever, of religious freedom. In order to address it in terms of the contemporary debate (complicated by the tremendous differences that the problem presents in democracies as opposed to dictatorships, in the more secularized countries as opposed to those of Muslim majority populations), it is useful to make a few cursory and therefore incomplete historical observations.

From the Catholic point of view it is also decisive

to refer to the teaching of the Second Vatican Council, contained in the declaration *Dignitatis Humanae* (December 7, 1965).

The Political Project of Imperial Restoration

In order to grasp the historical impact of the Edict of Milan, it is necessary to start with the process of transformation that began during the last two decades of the third century and the first two of the fourth, a transformation of epochal importance.[1]

Two political projects, one launched by Diocletian and the other by Constantine, mark this forty-year period. Both projects are characterized by a breadth that is "universal" (in terms of the Roman empire); one follows upon the other, but they are rather different in their intentions and results; they are situated at a historical, cultural, and religious juncture that is extremely variegated and complex, in which different currents of thought and action convey worldviews and objectives that often conflict.

Diocletian undertook the renovation of the empire beginning in 286, through an imposing administrative, political, and ideological reorganization involving an extensive and varied series of measures. Together with Maximian, he also decided to give a new impulse to the sacralization of the sovereigns (to whose *clementia* everyone paid the tribute of *adoratio*), promoting the affirmation of the absolute uniqueness of their relationship with the gods who ruled the empire: Jupiter and Hercules.[2]

The imperial ideology paired the emphasis of the sovereign figure with a series of elements aimed at fostering social and political cohesion, primarily by presenting once again the *mos maiorum* as the fundamental moral code of all the empire's inhabitants, capable of regulating every area of life, from the worship of the gods to marriage to relations between the emperors.

Diocletian's imperial renovation attempted to impose in the field of religion an obligatory point of convergence that would ensure the *pax deorum* and therefore the safety of the empire and its inhabitants in a decidedly variegated panorama in which the traditional cults were accompanied and sometimes overshadowed both by rituals derived from the Eastern mystery religions (like the cult of Mithra, which was fairly widespread in military circles) and by new syncretistic forms like Manichaeism (whose founder, Mani, had died in 277 AD).

The Persecution of Christians

The strongly theocratic character of the imperial renovation, with its presumption to apply to all of the empire's inhabitants, could not help but give rise to religious conflicts.[3]

The first to experience this outcome were the Manichaeans. Because of their refusal of military service, they were hit in 297 with an edict that defined as a serious crime the substitution of a new religion for the ancestral one, reviving the argument that there is greater value in the old than in the new, which had also been used extensively in the third century (for example, by the philosopher Porphyry) to belittle and denigrate the Christian *nouitas* and was well known to the Apologist Fathers.

In the same year, Diocletian began issuing measures aimed at Christians, initially limited to excluding them from the army. The true persecution began in 303, with the clear objective of a structural demolition of the Church: prohibition of the liturgical celebration, destruction of buildings of worship, confiscation of sacred books and furnishings. At the same time, the faithful were deprived of their recourse to the law and lost a series of personal rights and honors. Afterward the measures became more harsh. Ministers were incarcerated and forced to sacrifice to the gods; apostates were set free, and resisters were sentenced to death. Finally, a further tightening of the norms extended the same measures to all Christians.[4]

These repressive measures remained in effect until 311, although the intensity and duration of their application varied in the different parts of the empire. In the east there were several thousand martyrs and the persecution was more fierce, mainly because of the policies of Galerius and Maximinus II, while in the west the harassment practically ceased in 305 with the arrival of the second Tetrarchy and the ascent of Constantine.[5]

In light of the facts, Diocletian's ambitious plan proved inadequate in many respects: it failed to achieve the elimination of the dynastic system, the defense of the economy based on copper money (the *denarius*), and above all the hoped-for social cohesion.[6]

Defeat of the Policy of Repression

On April 30, 311, Galerius—who until that moment had distinguished himself by his relentless enforcement of the norms against Christians in the regions entrusted to him (which stretched from Thrace on the Black Sea to Greece and the northern part of Asia Minor)—issued an edict allowing Christians "to exist once again [*ut denuo sint*] and to rebuild their meeting places."[7] The emperor, who was seriously ill and near death, as his last act of governance recognized the existence of Christians and the lawfulness of their worship, but he did not give up on defending the correctness of his actions, aimed at bringing the Christians back to the *mos maiorum*. According to his view, the Christians had abandoned the institutions of their fathers because they were in the grip of a "great stubbornness and folly," to the point of deigning to make their own laws "as they pleased" and drawing others into their error; if now the imperial clemency permitted them to practice their Christian worship, this was only to prevent many inhabitants of the empire from living in a de facto atheism, in that they refused to offer the sacrifices prescribed by the sovereigns but were prevented from exercising their own faith.

This reveals the full extent of the anguish that had risen for Galerius, the heir of three centuries of relations between Roman power and Christianity: on the one hand he acknowledged that he had ultimately been defeated by events and recognized the fidelity of the Christians to their faith, as well as their capacity for proselytizing and attracting others; on the other he continued to maintain that it was an inalienable prerogative of imperial power to "manage" the relationship between the divine sphere and the subjects of the empire in pursuit of the *pax deorum* upon which the safety of the *res publica* depended. In his edict he presents as the sole conditions for the exercise of Christian worship that the faithful not do anything against public order and that they pray to "their God" for its safety, that of the empire, and their own (*"debebunt deum suum orare pro salute nostra, et reipublicae, ac sua"*).

From that moment the persecution came to an end almost everywhere in the empire.[8]

The Edict of Milan

The Revolution of Licinius and Constantine

Between the spring of 311 and that of 312, meanwhile, the conflict was growing between Constantine and Maxentius; it would culminate in the Battle of the Milvian Bridge (October 312) and conclude with Maxentius's death. During this time there occurred the "Constantinian revolution," the decision on the part of Constantine to entrust the fate of the empire—and his own fate as emperor—to the Christian God.[9] This decision was in complete continuity with the "charismatic" conception of power widely shared at the time, which made it indispensable, for the safety of the *res publica*, to seek an alliance with the divinity that would show itself to be stronger and more capable of granting victory, the sign of its benevolence toward the sovereign. What took place before the Battle of the Milvian Bridge, therefore, was exactly the culmination of the search for a *deus adiutor* in which Constantine had been engaged for some time.

It is not easy to discern—as some scholars attempt to do—to what extent the decision to entrust the good of the empire to the Christian God was, in addition to a political choice, also a sign of a personal conversion on the part of Constantine. And perhaps it is not even possible to do so in a methodologically correct way, if one begins on the basis of a "modern" view of the concepts of conversion, politics, and government.[10]

What is certain is that the victory of the Milvian Bridge confirmed for Constantine the decision he had made and impelled him to propose, in the meeting with the pagan Licinius in Milan in February of 313, the "institutionalization" of the relationship with the Christian God and his followers, guaranteeing in the first place the freedom of Christians to practice their religion throughout the empire.

The Initium Libertatis

"The Edict of Milan of 313 has an epochal significance because it marks the *initium libertatis* of modern man."[11] This statement by the illustrious scholar of Roman law Gabrio Lombardi makes it possible to identify how the provisions signed by the two Augusti, Constantine and Licinius, determined not only the gradual end of the persecution of Christians but above all—albeit within the objective limitations of the mentality of the time—the dawn of religious freedom. In fact, again in Lombardi's words, "in order that the freedom recognized in this sense for Christians should not appear as a sort of privilege, it was necessary to recognize it equally for all others, giving up on the intermingling of the 'juridical dimension' and the 'religious dimension' that had come down over a thousand years of history. This is why the text of the edict insists repeatedly that the freedom of conscience, of religion, of worship, was to be recognized not only for Christians but for all without distinction. And this is the first concrete clarification in history of the two dimensions that today we call 'religious freedom' and 'the secularism of the state': two dimensions that, in Western civilization, have become two aspects of a single prerequisite of the organizational experience of political society."[12] In a certain sense, in the Edict of Milan the two dimensions that today we call "religious freedom" and "secularism of the state" emerge for the first time in history as decisive factors in the good organization of political society.

The Letter from Licinius to the Governor of Bithynia

We do not have a direct and immediate account of the decisions made during the meeting between Constantine and Licinius on the occasion of the marriage between the sister of the former, Constantia, and the latter. Nevertheless, a letter of the summer of 313, sent by Licinius to the governor of Bithynia[13] and known also to Eusebius of Caesarea, specifies in view of their application the provisions concerning "all that pertains to safety and the public good," decided on the occasion of the "coming together" of the two

Augusti in Milan. The following is the text of the historic edict:

Perceiving long ago that religious liberty ought not to be denied, but that it ought to be granted to the judgment and desire of each individual to perform his religious duties according to his own choice, we had given orders that every man, Christians as well as others, should preserve the faith of his own sect and religion.

But since in that rescript, in which such liberty was granted them, many and various conditions seemed clearly added, some of them, it may be, after a little retired from such observance.

When I, Constantine Augustus, and I, Licinius Augustus, came under favorable auspices to Milan and took under consideration everything which pertained to the common good and prosperity, we resolved among other things, or rather first of all, to make such decrees as seemed in many respects for the benefit of every one; namely, such as should preserve reverence and piety toward the deity. We resolved, that is, to grant both to the Christians and to all men freedom to follow the religion which they choose, that whatever heavenly divinity exists may be propitious to us and to all that live under our government.

We have, therefore, determined, with sound and up-right purpose, that liberty is to be denied to no one, to choose and to follow the religious observances of the Christians, but that to each one freedom is to be given to devote his mind to that religion which he may think adapted to himself, in order that the Deity may exhibit to us in all things his accustomed care and favor.

It was fitting that we should write that this is our pleasure, that those conditions being entirely left out which were contained in our former letter concerning the Christians which was sent to your devotedness, everything that seemed very severe and foreign to our mildness may be annulled, and that now every one who has the same desire to observe the religion of the Christians may do so without molestation.

We have resolved to communicate this most fully to your care, in order that you may know that we have granted to these same Christians freedom and full liberty to observe their own religion.

Since this has been granted freely by us to them, your devotedness perceives that liberty is granted to others also who may wish to follow their own religious observances; it being clearly in accordance with the tranquillity of our times, that each one should have the liberty of choosing and worshiping whatever deity he pleases. This has been done by us in order that we might not seem in any way to discriminate against any rank or religion.

And we decree still further in regard to the Christians, that their places, in which they were formerly accustomed to assemble, and concerning which in the former letter sent to your devotedness a different command was given, if it appear that any have bought them either from our treasury or from any other person, shall be restored to the said Christians, without demanding money or any other equivalent, with no delay or hesitation.

If any happen to have received the said places as a gift, they shall restore them as quickly as possible to these same Christians: with the understanding that if those who have bought these places, or those who have received them as a gift, demand anything from our bounty, they may go to the judge of the district, that provision may be made for them by our clemency. All these things are to be granted to the society of Christians by your care immediately and without any delay.

And since the said Christians are known to have possessed not only those places in which they were accustomed to assemble, but also other places, belonging not to individuals among them, but to the society as a whole, that is, to the society of Christians, you will command that all these, in virtue of the law which we have above stated, be restored, without any hesitation, to these same Christians; that is, to their society and congregation: the above-mentioned provision being of course observed, that those who restore them without price, as we have before said, may expect indemnification from our bounty.

In all these things, for the benefit of the aforesaid society of Christians, you are to use the utmost diligence, to the end that our command may be speedily fulfilled, and that in this also, by our clemency, provision may be made for the common and public tranquillity.

For by this means, as we have said before, the divine favor toward us which we have already experienced in many matters will continue sure through all time.

And that the terms of this our gracious ordinance may be known to all, it is expected that this which we have written will be published everywhere by you and brought to the knowledge of all, in order that this gracious ordinance of ours may remain unknown to no one.[14]

The Innovations of the Edict

The promotion of the public good was for the two emperors made concrete in their agreeing upon the norms concerning respect for and veneration of the divinity (*diuinitatis reuerentia*) upon which the prosperity of the empire depended. The priority appeared to be ensuring that "no one be denied the ability to follow and to choose the observance or worship of the Christians; and that everyone be given the ability to apply himself to that cult which he maintained to be suited to himself" (*ut daremus et christianis et omnibus liberam potestatem sequendi religionem quam quisque uoluisset*), so that "the divinity might bestow in everything its usual solicitude and benevolence" (*quo quicquid est diuinitatis in sede caelesti . . . placatum ac propitium possit existere*). This formulation, clearly the fruit of the conference between the two Augusti, makes even more significant the emphasis given to the Christians, as admission of the fact that they were, *in primis*, the subjects to be protected.

The edict, without exceeding the ideological framework of its time, presents interesting innovations: while the *pax deorum* remains the rulers' main preoccupation, there is a complete disappearance of every reference that might identify the emperors with the divinity; moreover, religious freedom no longer appears as a magnanimous concession of imperial pardon in the face of the arrogant willfulness of certain men, but rather the recognition of the absolute freedom of the divinity itself in requiring the modalities of worship and the sovereign's renunciation of the power to decide which *religio* might be *licita* and which not.[15]

This change in terminology contains a precise judgment of value. With the famous Edict of Milan, the emperor granted to the inhabitants of the empire, the Christians and everyone else, a measure of religious freedom. The scope of the provisions raises the awareness that God interacts with human history. In fact, with the edict of 313, Constantine opened to Christianity the popular masses.

In reference to the consequences of the Edict of Milan, Eusebius of Caesarea writes: "And finally a bright and splendid day, overshadowed by no cloud, illuminated with beams of heavenly light the churches of Christ throughout the entire world. And not even those without our communion were prevented from sharing in the same blessings, or at least from coming under their influence and enjoying a part of the benefits bestowed upon us by God. All men, then, were freed from the oppression of the tyrants, and being released from the former ills, one in one way and another in another acknowledged the defender of the pious to be the only true God. And we especially who placed our hopes in the Christ of God had unspeakable gladness . . ."[16]

2

The Long Travail
of Religious Freedom

Historical Notes

In the Edict of Milan we find for the first time, albeit with limitations, a socio-juridical expression of religious freedom. Nonetheless, one cannot deny that the Edict of Milan was a sort of "spoiled beginning." The events that followed, in fact, opened a long and tumultuous history. In the relationship between state and Church there soon arose two mutual temptations: for the state that of using the Church as an *instrumentum regni*, and for the Church that of using the state as an *instrumentum salvationis*.[17]

The undue historical intermingling of political power and religion heavily influenced the different phases through which the practice of religious freedom passed. Simply reviewing the major events of the seventeen centuries between the Edict of Milan and the present day should allow one to grasp the grave contradictions connected to the practice, and even to the conception, of religious freedom.[18]

Although the Edict of Milan constitutes a *novum* in the ancient context, we cannot call it more than an antecedent of religious freedom in the modern sense. In particular following the wars of religion, modernity understands religious freedom as a *right of the subject*, which was unknown in antiquity (until the voluntarism of the late Middle Ages). For the *ancient* it is the "religious sphere" that is free; for the *modern* it is the "subject who exercises his freedom" in religious matters.

From Justinian to Saint Augustine

Let us review the evolution of imperial legislation from the fourth century to the fifth: from the declaration of religious freedom that permitted the Church to live and develop in the open,[19] moving through the strange experiment of Julian the Apostate,[20] we arrive at the adoption of Catholicism as the "religion of the state."

Without denying the involutional character of the edict of Theodosius to Thessalonica of February 27, 380, it must be evaluated in light of its context: unlike in the preceding period, the threats to the peace of the empire did not come mainly from disputes with the pagans, but rather from doctrinal disputes within Christianity; it was the phenomenon of the heretics that created social disorder.[21] This edict was afterward incorporated into the code of Justinian with greater prominence. It would become, in fact, the *incipit* of the whole compilation: the *Codex* opens with a section entitled *"De Summa Trinitate et de fide catholica et ut nemo de ea publice contendere audeat."*[22]

In this context Saint Ambrose, who came from a career as an important state official (*consularis*) and was an expert in juridical-administrative problems, does not hesitate to remind Christians to be loyal to the civil authority that, in turn, was responsible for guaranteeing the freedom of citizens. In the context of the public good to which citizens and authority must contribute, he demonstrates a strong awareness of the state, which does not, however, prevent him from opposing and condemning the morally reprehensible actions of the emperor, to the point of imposing canonical penalties on him.[23]

Even more significant is Ambrose's dispute with the authorities over their concession of a basilica to the new Arian bishop of the city. He went to the building and, supported by the crowd outside, argued that basilicas belonged not to the emperor but to the Church. Later the people would occupy a basilica (the *basilica nova*) to defend it from imperial and military claims, and the Milanese bishop himself would go there to preach.[24] It is clear in this situation how the question of the "heretics," a source of social disorder, generated serious difficulties for the development of religious freedom.

Augustine is a paradigmatic example of the growing complexity of the theory and practice of religious freedom. His exegesis of the words *"compelle intrare"* in the parable of the banquet (see Luke 14:16–24) is the result of a radical change of attitude attested to by the bishop of Hippo himself in a very famous letter, written between 407 and 408, to the schismatic bishop Vincentius: I have therefore yielded to the evidence afforded by these instances which my colleagues have laid before me. For originally my opinion was that no one should be coerced into the unity of Christ, that we must act only by words, fight only by arguments, and prevail by force of reason, lest we should have those whom we knew as avowed heretics feigning themselves to be Catholics. But this opinion of mine was overcome not by the words of those who controverted it, but by the conclusive instances to which they could point. For, in the first place, there was set over against my opinion my own town, which, although it was once wholly on the side of Donatus, was brought over to the Catholic unity by fear of the imperial edicts, but which we now see filled with such detestation of your ruinous perversity, that it would scarcely be believed that it had ever been involved in your error. There were so many others which were mentioned to me by name, that, from facts themselves, I was made to own that to this matter the word of Scripture might be understood as applying: "Give opportunity to a wise man, and he will be yet wiser." (Proverbs 9:9) For how many were already, as we assuredly know, willing to be Catholics, being moved by the indisputable plainness of truth, but daily putting off their avowal of this through fear of offending their own party! How many were bound, not by truth—for you never pretended to that as yours—but by the heavy chains of inveterate custom, so that in them was fulfilled the divine saying: "A servant (who is hardened) will not be corrected by words; for though he understand, he will not answer"! (Proverbs 29:19) How many supposed the sect of Donatus to be the true Church, merely because ease had made them too listless, or conceited, or sluggish, to take pains to examine Catholic truth! How many would have entered earlier had not the calumnies of slanderers, who declared that we offered something else than we do upon the altar of God, shut them out! How many, believing that it mattered not to which party a Christian might belong, remained in the schism of Donatus only because they had been born in it, and no one was compelling them to forsake it and pass over into the Catholic Church![25]

In the face of this strong stance taken by the bishop of Hippo, it must be said that some of the Church fathers recognized the difficulties that such a stance created for the Church. It is no coincidence that Saint Jerome came to the point of writing: "Since the Church has had Catholic emperors, it has certainly grown in power and in wealth, but it has diminished in moral force."[26]

In any case one must recognize, as for the topic in question, that the Augustinian exegesis remained "a maxim that for many centuries would inform some stances of churchmen and would encourage the encounter of those two reciprocal temptations which we indicated above."[27]

From the Middle Ages to the Wars of Religion

The Christian Middle Ages were characterized by a substantially Catholic civilization, with intellectual features taken from the faith even when its principles were not always and systematically lived and realized.

This is the time of tension between the empire and the Church, and of the fight for the *libertas Ecclesiae*; the outcome would sometimes be tipped in favor of political power, sometimes in favor of ecclesiastical. But more significant for the evolution of the idea of religious freedom is the treatment that was reserved for the heretics. Their sentencing to death "was something normal until the 16th century and in some countries until the 17th, and was not limited to Catholic regions of the world. The burning of heretics was practiced by the political authorities but it was the ecclesiastical authority that sentenced them and handed them over to the state."[28]

Thomas Aquinas himself, while he firmly rejects

the use of force to obtain the conversion of Jews and Gentiles (this should be interpreted as referring to the followers of Islam), has no difficulty admitting the practice of repression, to the point of death, with regard to heretics who are not disposed for conversion: "Among unbelievers there are some who have never received the faith, such as the heathens and the Jews: and these are by no means to be compelled to the faith, in order that they may believe, because to believe depends on the will: nevertheless they should be compelled by the faithful, if it be possible to do so, so that they do not hinder the faith, by their blasphemies, or by their evil persuasions, or even by their open persecutions. It is for this reason that Christ's faithful often wage war with unbelievers, not indeed for the purpose of forcing them to believe, because even if they were to conquer them, and take them prisoners, they should still leave them free to believe, if they will, but in order to prevent them from hindering the faith of Christ. On the other hand, there are unbelievers who at some time have accepted the faith, and professed it, such as heretics and all apostates: such should be submitted even to bodily compulsion, that they may fulfill what they have promised, and hold what they, at one time, received."[29]

With the passing of time, inroads were made into European culture—in part through discussions on the relationship between council and pope, the attempts at reunification with the East, and the works of the humanists of the fifteenth and sixteenth centuries—by a certain position that began to look at "human experience in purely immanentist terms."[30]

The paradox of European history in this period is that the development of the Protestant Reformation, in its variegated expressions (Waldensian, Lutheran, Calvinist, and the form proper to the Anglican community), far from fostering a recovery of "religious freedom," led to a tightening of the bonds between political power and religious power that would result in the wars of religion.

In order to resolve this situation, the Peace of Augsburg (1555) and the Peace of Westphalia (1648) recognized the principle *"cuius regio, eius et religio,"*[31] which required that the subject conform to the religion of his prince. This dominated, at least in its general outlines, the history of the modern state, which founded its political unity and stability on religion, considered an indispensable factor of social cohesion. This principle, however, was unable to overcome the critical intermingling of political power and religion and merely circumscribed it within the limits of the nation-states. Political borders, therefore, also enclosed the religious confession, which was required to be that of the prince: once again the state imposed its own faith.

"Modern" Religious Freedom and the Pontifical Magisterium of the Nineteenth Century

In this juridical context, the weakening of the idea of "religious freedom" corresponds to a strengthening of the concept of "tolerance" (which, however, does not in any way contemplate religious indifferentism).

The modern result of Europe's tumultuous history with regard to the relationship between state and religions would be the configuration of states that ignore the religious dimension, making it an exclusively private individual question.

The claim of the ethical state would then be imposed, leading to the totalitarianism of the twentieth century. In various forms, the reduction of the scope of democracy purely to the relationship between the state and the individual citizen would also spread, in the ignorance, not rarely complete, of civil society and of the social subjects that inhabit it.[32]

On the American continent this approach took on a profoundly different tone, partly because of the influence of the thought of John Locke, who in his *Letter Concerning Toleration* of 1689 clearly affirms that religious faith is a private affair of citizens and must be considered such by the state, which has no jurisdiction in this regard.[33] The juridical picture of the emerging United States, expressed in the 1776 Virginia Declaration of Rights, thus differentiates itself on one fundamental point from the 1789 Declaration of the Rights of Man, an expression of the French Revolution. Both texts establish a principle of religious freedom, but while the French one is stated in opposition to the old order, the American one is conceived in a clearly positive vein, by virtue of respect for the Creator and freedom of conscience.[34]

Within this modern setting, let us seek to understand the content and expressions of the pontifical magisterium with regard to freedom of conscience through the nineteenth century and until the promulgation of the *Dignitatis Humanae* at the end of the Second Vatican Council.[35]

The popes, in the context of modernity, condemned the system of freedom of conscience and of worship resulting from the French declaration of 1789.[36] The reasons for such a position must be sought above all in the ideological sources of the declaration: the natural-law approach of the Enlightenment and rationalism, the thought of Rousseau, and the influence of the notorious Civil Constitution of the Clergy, with which the revolutionary Assemblée had overturned the relationship between state and Church. Pius VI criticized the conception of absolute moral freedom proposed by the French declaration. Gregory XVI, addressing the famous case of Lamennais in the encyclical *Mirari Vos*, disapproved of indifferentism and the absolute freedom of conscience founded upon it. Finally, Pius IX in the famous documents *Quanta Cura* and *Syllabus* would deplore political and philosophical naturalism and the freedom of conscience and worship connected to it.

This is obviously not the place to go beyond this general overview. We will limit ourselves to endorsing the balanced view presented by the Spanish theologian Gerardo del Pozo Abejón at the end of his rigorous analysis: "Pius VI, Gregory XVI, and Pius IX opposed secularism and the proclamation of the autonomy of the individual and society in relation to God and to his Church. But they did not deny the freedom that every man must enjoy with regard to the state in order to seek the truth about God, precisely because they did not take this freedom into consideration. At the most they condemned the right to any religious practice whatsoever in the civil sphere. Another question is the fact that these popes spoke on the basis of the juridical-ecclesiological theory of the indirect power of the Church over the state, abandoned by Vatican II."[37]

3

Dignitatis Humanae

Is it possible to identify in the magisterium of the popes following Pius IX any doctrinal elements that may have opened the way to *Dignitatis Humanae*, the declaration of the Second Vatican Council on religious freedom that Paul VI promulgated in 1965? In the twentieth century Catholic tradition began to depart from the classical doctrine on the freedom of the act of faith and, in social terms, from that on tolerance and evolve toward the elaboration of the fundamental duties and rights of the person, which the state must not only respect but also serve. We therefore began to see a shifting of perspective from the rights of the "truth" to the rights of the "person."[38]

In his time Leo XIII was already taking an open stance in defense of the fundamental rights of man.[39] With reference to his predecessors the pontiff of *Rerum Novarum* moved in continuity and progress, "continuity, because he continued to condemn theoretical indifferentism at both the individual and the social level, the positive authorization on the part of the law of such indifferentism, and the resulting freedom without limits. Progress, because he distinguished—and thus avoided confusion—between freedom of conscience founded on indifferentism and true freedom of conscience with regard to the state in order to pursue, in conscience, the will of God and to fulfill his commandments without any obstacle."[40]

After him, Pius XI was led by the tragedy of totalitarianism to a strenuous and systematic defense of the dignity, freedom, and rights of the human person. The two key points of his magisterium are on the one hand the existence of a universal moral order and on the other the centrality, dignity, and fundamental rights of man as person. These teachings objectively opened the way to the affirmation of the right to religious freedom. Pius XII, following the 1948 Universal Declaration of Human Rights, revisited this topic in the discourse *Ci riesce* of 1953. Finally, John XXIII in the encyclical *Pacem in Terris* insisted on the human right to venerate God according to one's upright conscience.

The Promulgation of *Dignitatis Humanae*

The promulgation of *Dignitatis Humanae* was therefore the culmination of a gradual and decisive evolution.[41] In order to be understood correctly, however, the declaration must be placed in the general context of the magisterium of Vatican II, in that "pastoral nature" that finds its emblematic expression in the constitution *Gaudium et Spes*.[42] This constitution offered *Dignitatis Humanae* two fundamental coordinates: a new understanding of the relationship between the Church and the political community, and the recognition of the dignity and freedom of the human person. This was a sign of the times that led to a vision of the person as principle, subject, and end of all social institutions.

What are the fundamental innovations of the conciliar teaching? They are found above all in section 2 of the declaration: This Vatican Council declares that the human person has a right to religious freedom. This freedom means that all men are to be immune from coercion on the part of individuals or of social groups and of any human power, that no one is to be forced to act in a manner contrary to his own beliefs, whether privately or publicly, whether alone or in association with others, within due limits. The council further declares that the right to religious freedom has its foundation in the very dignity of the human person as this dignity is known through the revealed word of God and by reason itself. This right of the human person to religious freedom is to be recognized in the constitutional law whereby society is governed and thus it is to become a civil right. It is in accordance with their dignity as persons—that is, beings endowed with reason and free will and therefore privileged to bear personal responsibility—that all men should be at once impelled by nature and also bound by a moral obligation to seek the truth, especially religious truth. They are also bound to adhere to the truth, once it is known, and to order their whole lives in accord with the demands of truth. However, men cannot discharge these obligations in a manner in keeping with their own nature unless they enjoy immunity from external coercion as well as psychological freedom. Therefore the right to religious freedom has its foundation not in the subjective disposition of the person, but in his very nature. In consequence, the right to this immunity continues to exist even in those who do not live up to their obligation of seeking the truth and adhering to it, and the exercise of this right is not to be impeded, provided that just public order be observed.[43]

The Innovations of Conciliar Teaching

In speaking of religious freedom in these terms, the council, in the light of right reason, autonomous in itself but confirmed and illuminated by divine revelation, refers not in general terms to moral freedom with regard to the truth or to a value but specifically to juridical freedom in the area of social and interpersonal relations. It is, moreover, important to specify that at this level the right of which we are speaking is a negative right that establishes the limits of the state and of civil power, denying them direct jurisdiction over religious choice. Understood in this way, the right to religious freedom implies immunity from

coercion in a twofold sense: man has the right not to
be forced to act against his conscience and not to be
prevented from acting in conformity with it. This
creates "a safety zone that guarantees the inviolabil-
ity of the human space."[44] The only limitation recognized in the exercise of this right is respect for the
"public order informed by justice."[45] In the conciliar
declaration the classical doctrine of tolerance is superseded by the recognition that "the human person
has the right to religious freedom" and that this right
"endures even in those who do not satisfy the obligation of seeking the truth and adhering to it." With
lucidity and concision, Nikolaus Lobkowicz, a former
rector of the University of Munich and president of
the Catholic University of Eichstätt, affirms that "the
extraordinary quality of the declaration *Dignitatis Humanae* consists in its having transferred the issue of
religious freedom from the notion of truth to that
of the rights of the human person. If error has no
rights, a person has rights even when he errs. Clearly
this is not a matter of a right before God; it is a right
with respect to other persons, the community, and
the state."[46] This conclusion is the result, as we have
stated, of a tremendous effort to establish an adequate
anthropology.

Turning again to del Pozo Abejón, let us empha-
size one aspect of the richness of the conciliar teaching on religious freedom. The juridical and negative
character of this freedom is rather far from an absolute and unlimited conception of moral freedom (in
perfect continuity with the traditional doctrine); at
the same time, however, it brings out clearly the anthropological impact of the social dimension of religious freedom: *Dignitatis Humanae* demonstrates the
need to think out thoroughly "the juridical" when one
wishes to reflect on the dignity of the human person.

Here is del Pozo Abejón's concise and illuminating summary of the conciliar teaching: "[The] right
to religious freedom in *Dignitatis Humanae* is not a
right to profess an erroneous religion, but rather the
right not to be prevented from adopting a position
in religious matters; that is, it is a negative right: its
object is not the content of religion, nor the presumed
error, nor any action of the active subject of the same
right, but rather the immunity from external coercion,
the creation of an inviolable social buffer zone of non-
intervention by the state or any other social subject, in
which every man can satisfy the need to act according
to his own initiative and responsibility, and not to be
hindered from the outside in his particular choices.

The space in which the right must be exercised includes not only the private, but also the public; not only the practice of worship, but also of expression. . . . And this is not a matter of a right whose source would be positive civil legislation, but rather of a fundamental or natural right whose source is the human person, his rational nature, his free will and responsibility; a natural right that must be recognized civilly."[47]

The Magisterium of John Paul II and of Benedict XVI

On September I, 1980, in the wake of the conciliar declaration, Blessed John Paul II sent a historic message to the heads of state who had signed the final statement of the Helsinki Conference on Security and Co-operation.[48] In it he presented in a detailed manner the "specific elements corresponding to the concept of 'religious freedom'" and emphasized the "closely interrelated individual and community aspects, private and public." On that occasion he did not limit himself to exploring the impact of the teaching of the council on this matter but highlighted the fact that it cannot be reduced merely to the theoretical horizon of liberalism.[49] The freedom of religion, conscience, and conversion is not foreign to the legal framework nor to the common mentality of Western countries, but it is generally burdened by a twofold reduction. On the one hand conscience is conceived of in terms that we can call "creative" in the sense of being mistaken,[50] meaning that it is capable of defining on its own what is good and what is evil; on the other this freedom is attributed exclusively to the individual, relegated to the domain of the private and prevented from carrying out a public function of any significance.

In conclusion, begging the pardon of every sort of traditionalism, we can affirm that *Dignitatis Humanae* constitutes a paradigmatic example of re-sourcement, a return to the sources. In it the Church, in fact, overcoming misunderstandings and abandoning mistaken paths, is recovering with greater awareness and power a doctrine that right reason recognizes as an expression of human dignity and that finds full confirmation in Christian revelation.[51]

In this regard we present the words that in 2005 Benedict XVI, in the context of a discourse on the correct hermeneutic of the Second Vatican Council, dedicated to *Dignitatis Humanae*:

Thus, for example, if religious freedom were to be considered an expression of the human inability to discover the truth and thus become a canonization of relativism, then this social and historical necessity is raised inappropriately to the metaphysical level and thus stripped of its true meaning. Consequently, it cannot be accepted by those who believe that the human person is capable of knowing the truth about God and, on the basis of the inner dignity of the truth, is bound to this knowledge.

It is quite different, on the other hand, to perceive religious freedom as a need that derives from human coexistence, or indeed, as an intrinsic consequence of the truth that cannot be externally imposed but that the person must adopt only through the process of conviction.

The Second Vatican Council, recognizing and making its own an essential principle of the modern State with the Decree on Religious Freedom, has recovered the deepest patrimony of the Church. By so doing she can be conscious of being in full harmony with the teaching of Jesus himself (cf. Mt 22:21), as well as with the Church of the martyrs of all time. The ancient Church naturally prayed for the emperors and political leaders out of duty (cf. I Tm 2:2); but while she prayed for the emperors, she refused to worship them and thereby clearly rejected the religion of the State.

The martyrs of the early Church died for their faith in that God who was revealed in Jesus Christ, and for this very reason they also died for freedom of conscience and the freedom to profess one's own faith—a profession that no State can impose but which, instead, can only be claimed with God's grace in freedom of conscience. A missionary Church known for proclaiming her message to all peoples must necessarily work for the freedom of the faith. She desires to transmit the gift of the truth that exists for one and all.

At the same time, she assures peoples and their Governments that she does not wish to destroy their identity and culture by doing so, but to give them, on the contrary, a response which, in their innermost depths, they are waiting for—a response with which the multiplicity of cultures is not lost but instead unity between men and women increases and thus also peace between peoples.[52]

4

Thought and Practice

In the lives of men and societies, as in the life of the Church, the acquisition of a renewed understanding of the truth always constitutes the beginning of a journey rather than a point of arrival. This law is not suspended for the affirmation of religious freedom as it is proposed to us by the declaration *Dignitatis Humanae*.[53]

Some Worrying Facts

Speaking of religious freedom today means confronting an emergency that is increasingly global in character. According to the careful study of Brian J. Grim and Roger Finke, in the period between 2000 and

2007 there were 123 countries in which some form of religious persecution took place, and unfortunately the number is constantly on the rise.[54]

Violent Persecution

Rapidly reviewing the countries of the world, one must immediately note the radical difference between true violent persecution of all those who profess a faith different from the official one and harassment perpetrated in more subtle forms.[55]

It is well known that many violations of religious freedom occur in Africa and Asia, and in particular in countries with majority Muslim populations. Significantly, scholars like Olivier Roy maintain that it is precisely around religious freedom that many of the tensions of Muslim societies are catalyzed, as they gradually abandon their traditional configuration.[56] Therefore, in countries where a state religion still dominates, where the value of state religious neutrality has not yet been discovered, promoting religious freedom means primarily encouraging religious pluralism and openness to all religious expressions, beginning with the abrogation of laws that sometimes even criminalize blasphemy.[57]

On the other hand, in countries where dictatorial regimes of atheist origin are still installed, the persecution of dissidents and those belonging to religious communities continues to be a common practice. It should suffice to cite the beginning of the long section dedicated to China in Aid to the Church in Need's latest report on religious freedom: "2011 was characterized by an enormous number of violations of human rights and religious freedom. Never as in this year has there been such a long list of arrests among Christians (Catholics and Protestants), Muslims, Buddhists (Tibetans), but also among dissidents, human rights advocates, activists for democracy, bloggers, artists (like Ai Weiwei), journalists."[58]

The European West

Examining realities closer to us, more than the risk of violent persecution it appears urgent to overcome the latent mistrust of the phenomenon of religion. Such mistrust is inherent in the inadequacy of some conceptions of secularism, which end up generating a climate unfavorable to authentic religious freedom.

In this regard, the Observatory on Intolerance and Discrimination against Christians in Europe has drawn up a worrying list of events that took place on our continent in 2011: acts of discrimination or the denial of rights (attacks on freedom of expression, freedom of conscience, the freedom of parents with regard to raising their children, or the institutional or collective dimension of religious freedom and discriminatory "equality" policies); acts of intolerance or marginalization (exclusion of Christians from public and social life, exclusion of Christian symbols from the public sphere; social disadvantages for Christians, insults and defamation, misrepresentation of Christians in the mass media through negative stereotyping); and incidents of hatred (crimes against persons, interruptions of religious services, acts of vandalism).[59]

It must also be recognized that there are now numerous and frequent judicial decisions in the West that tend to restrict the full expression of religious freedom: from the ban on conscientious objection in the professional sphere, to the prohibition on wearing or displaying religious symbols, to the obligatory teaching, even in schools of religious inspiration, of material based on an anthropology contrary to one's own creed.

The Situation in the United States

One particular case occupied the pages of the press on the occasion of the recent presidential election: the debate over religious freedom in the United States. The reason was the introduction by the Obama administration of regulations for implementing the recent health-care reform that require various kinds of religious institutions (in particular, hospitals and schools) to offer their employees health insurance policies that cover contraception, abortion, and sterilization procedures. The Department of Health and Human Services (HHS) decided to grant exemptions only to institutions that define themselves as churches in the strict sense or that provide services exclusively to fellow members of their religion. The dioceses of the United States, however, manage vast educational and health-care networks. They are therefore presented with a choice between violating Catholic moral teaching and separating themselves formally from works that are the result of centuries of effort, with the grave risk that these "ex-Catholic" schools or hospitals would then conform to the standards dictated by the administration. Moreover, juridically nondiocesan Catholic institutions too would find themselves either violating Catholic moral doctrine or paying severe financial penalties (one hundred dollars per day per employee, under the regulations proposed). Their very existence would in fact be compromised.

In various statements the bishops of the United States have openly affirmed that the HHS mandate is unacceptable primarily for three reasons.[60] The first is that with it the government has claimed for itself the right to define what is a religious institution and has done so in an absurdly restrictive sense, leaving out all of the social works that Catholics consider an integral part of the proclamation of the Gospel. The second is that the HHS mandate forces institutions that it considers "nonreligious" to violate their own moral and religious teachings. The third is that it also violates the consciences of individual believers, forcing them to act against their most sincere convictions. This third point has raised a great deal of surprise and criticism because the bishops are seen as having implicitly affirmed a right to conscientious objection not only for religious institutions but also for all Catholic employers. In the rather heated debate that has arisen, many commentators, including the bishops, have spoken of attacks on religious freedom.

Critical Aspects of Religious Freedom

These facts, the expression of a grave disorder of civilization, demand an exploration of this issue without overlooking the debates (sometimes heated and never put to rest) on the nature, correct interpretation, and necessary adoption of *Dignitatis Humanae*. Our reflection will now focus on some aspects of the issue relevant to constitutional democracies of the more prosperous regions of the planet.

A Complex Knot of "Classical" Problems

The issue of "religious freedom," which at first glance raises a very widespread consensus, has always possessed a content that is anything but obvious. It is embedded, in fact, in a fairly complex knot in which at least three serious problems intersect: (a) the relationship between objective truth and individual conscience, (b) the coordination between religious communities and state power, and (c) from the Christian theological viewpoint, the interpretation of the universality of salvation in Christ in the face of the plurality of religions and worldviews ("substantive" ethical visions).

One cannot reasonably deny that the text of the conciliar declaration is in itself very clear, that this freedom is objectively implied by an adequate anthropology, and that the sense in which it is affirmed is perfectly consistent with Christian revelation. This does not change the fact, however, that this is a complex concept and that speaking of "limits" on this freedom, not to mention its coexistence with the duty of the subject to seek the truth, brings into play a network of relationships whose balance is not settled once and for all.

Decisive New Questions

These "classical" problems of the interpretation of religious freedom are joined today by new questions that are no less decisive. The first is the relationship between the personal religious quest and its community expression. The question is often raised: Can religious freedom be limited to a solely individual expression?

Moreover, one must ask under what conditions a "religious group" can claim public recognition in an interreligious and intercultural society. We are facing the delicate issue of the power of the legitimately constituted public authority to distinguish what is an authentic religion and what is not. This clearly confirms that the distinction between political power and religions/worldviews is not as obvious as it might first appear, above all when the dominant culture interprets the religious phenomenon more and more as personal self-realization and less and less as belonging to pre-existing traditions and communities.[61]

Religions and Sects

The problem of the distinction between religions and "sects" is similar. The issue is as ancient as the Roman notion of *religio licita*, but recently it has become much sharper, above all because of the fragmentation and proliferation of "communities" within the Christian world and because of the agnostic position of most legislation dealing with matters of religious connotation, together with the preservation of a certain favoritism with regard to religious communities. The sociological indicators that identify a "sect" establish a continuum between sectarian and nonsectarian groups, in which the latter extreme is occupied by the most "casual" and secularized forms of religious membership, making it very difficult to draw a precise dividing line.

Freedom of Conversion

To these problems, which are already very delicate, must be added a question that has lately become particularly burning: that of freedom of conversion.[62] Although it cannot be said that this problem is new, it has certainly taken on greater visibility with respect to other time periods.

For all of these reasons, thinking about and practicing religious freedom today appears much more difficult than one might expect, especially after the conciliar declaration. It must be acknowledged frankly that speaking about religious freedom today is rather arduous. This is not, in fact, simply a matter of elaborating an anthropological (and, in the Christian sense, theological) reflection but also of adequately taking into account widely varying social and political expressions that behave like moving targets.

5

Knots to Untie

Within this context, in order to untie some of the problematic knots it is useful and appropriate to make at least two kinds of considerations.

Beginning with an understanding of religious freedom as the absence of external constraint in matters of worship and belief, the affirmations of *Dignitatis Humanae* still appear relevant and complete in their genre. However, the decades since then have brought to light two serious new problems (among others).

Religious Freedom and Social Peace

The first concerns the connection between *religious freedom and social peace*. Not only practice but also various recent studies have highlighted the very close connection between the two realities.[63] Abstractly speaking, one could imagine that legislation capable of decreasing religious diversity could also reduce or even eliminate the conflict that can stem from it, but in fact exactly the opposite is true: the more strictures the state imposes, the more religiously motivated conflict increases. In reality this result is understandable: imposing or prohibiting religious practices by law, besides the obvious improbability of modifying the corresponding personal beliefs, does nothing other than increase the resentment and frustration that is afterward manifested in public as conflict.

Religious Freedom and the Stance of Public Institutions

The second problem is even more complex and requires a more extensive reflection. It concerns the connection between *religious freedom* and the *stance taken by the state*—and, on various levels, all public institutions—with regard to religious communities in civil society.

The Evolution of
Democratic-Liberal Societies

The evolution of democratic-liberal societies has increasingly changed the balance on which public authority was traditionally based. There has been a decline of shared anthropological structures and values, which were external to the legal structure but acted as axiological presuppositions, according to Böckenförde's famous principle on the foundation of the liberal state ("The liberal and secularized state feeds on normative premises that it cannot generate by itself")[64] and the considerations on justice presented by Michael Sandel.[65] Traditionally the state needed to do nothing other than "recognize" rights, values, and realities that existed in the social ethos, limiting itself to regulating their most significant consequences for associative political life. It escapes no one that this position depended on the awareness, peacefully possessed, of the radical insufficiency of the idea of a "pure right." Until a few decades ago, the substantial and explicit reference went to generally recognized anthropological structures, at least in the broad sense, as derived from the religious tradition: birth, marriage, reproduction, education, death. This is why even intentionally "anticlerical" legislation bore within itself an extensive echo of Christian religious values and why the problem of the ultimate foundation of the law was hardly relevant politically.

From Moral Judgment of Legislation to Religious Freedom

What happened when this point of reference of religious origin was brought into question and ultimately seen as unusable? Contemporary neoliberalism moved toward positions that seek to base politics on procedures that are entirely neutral with respect to any "substantive" vision, wanting to guarantee active neutrality but in some cases even coming to the point of theorizing that those who believe in a truth must simply be excluded from the liberal political debate, as maintained by philosopher Richard Rorty, an author of no small influence: "We heirs of the Enlightenment think of enemies of liberal democracy like Nietzsche

or Loyola as, to use Rawls's word, 'mad.' We do so because there is no way to see them as fellow citizens of
our constitutional democracy, people whose life plans
might, given ingenuity and good will, be fitted in with
those of other citizens. They are not crazy because
they have mistaken the ahistorical nature of human
beings. They are crazy because the limits of sanity
are set by what *we* can take seriously."[66] In comparison
with these words, those of Benedict XVI on the "dic-
tatorship of relativism" appear to be an understate-
ment.[67]

In this way, through recoil, the classical problem
of moral judgment on legislation has increasingly been
turning into a problem of religious freedom. Obviously we are simply considering that which, according
to many authors, has taken place. That is, we would
like to describe a factual historical situation, or at
least a tendency that is widespread in the pluralist societies of the West.

A Theoretical Presupposition

The theoretical presupposition of this evolution does
not surpass, in point of fact, the rigidity of the French
model of *laïcité*, based on the idea that state institutions

ought to be "indifferent" or "neutral" with respect to the phenomenon of religion, as they are deemed unfit to construct a favorable environment for the religious freedom of all. This is a conception that, beyond reference to the specific French model, is widespread in the juridical and political culture of the West, in particular within European institutions. It is a conception that, interpreting the categories of religious freedom in light of the so-called neutrality of the state, instead of protecting an irreducible distinction ends up becoming an institutional prejudice against the phenomenon of religion.[68]

Neutrality?

The very idea of "neutrality," in fact, is rather problematic, above all because it is not applicable to civil society, the precedence of which the state must always respect, being deputized to "govern" it and not to "manage" it.[69] However, respecting civil society requires recognition of a new objective fact: today in Western civil societies, above all those of Europe, the most profound divisions are those between the secularist culture and the religious phenomenon, and not—as is often erroneously thought—among believers of different faiths. The intention here is simply to recognize this fact, and not to underestimate the tragic burden of fundamentalism and the beneficial contribution of the "polyarchies." Otherwise, the just and necessary aconfessionality of the state based on the idea of "neutrality" ends up legitimizing a vision of public authority as defender of a secularism foreign to religious realities and mistrustful, if not discriminatory, toward them. In other words, the conception of the state in terms of neutrality favors the identification—often found more in practice than in theory—of *secular* with *nonreligious*, in such a way that the public sphere becomes predisposed to harmonize itself with all of the different visions and practices except those of religion: by virtue of this unacknowledged cultural prejudice, while all the different positions are considered legitimate parts of variegated contemporary pluralism, those of religion are instead perceived as partisan differences. In this way the so-called neutral state is not culturally impartial but takes on a secularist orientation that, through legislative choices, above all in anthropologically sensitive matters, becomes hostile toward cultural identities of religious origin. Through the objectivity and authoritativeness of the law is spread—in fact—a culture marked by a secularized vision of man and of the world, which is legitimate as one voice in a pluralistic society but which the state cannot make its own without assuming implicitly an undue substantive position that restricts religious freedom. Even in a country like Italy, which in its own constitution and the practice of its courts does not assert French *laïcité* but proposes a collaborative *laicità*,[70] there is no lack of indications of such a tendency.[71]

Religious Neutrality of the State and Renewed Thought on Religious Freedom

How can this grave state of affairs be remedied?

Of course, everything cannot be left to politics, even if one must not underestimate the influence of some ideological decisions that are claimed to be cutting edge and deputized to educate the common mentality: it is not always true that the laws respond to real needs of civil society.

In order to offer an alternative and constructive proposal to this state of affairs, one must rethink the issue of the aconfessionality of the state in the context of renewed thinking on religious freedom. What is needed is a state that, without making any specific vision its own, does not interpret its aconfessionality as "detachment," as an impossible neutralization of the worldviews that are expressed in civil society, but opens spaces in which each personal and social subject may make its own contribution to the common good.[72]

Freedom of Religion?

It is nonetheless appropriate to ask oneself: is the best way to confront this delicate situation to claim freedom of religion for the different communities, asking respect for the "peculiarities" of all the minority moral sensibilities? By itself this request, even if it is legitimate, nevertheless risks reinforcing in the public square the idea that the religious identity is made up of nothing but obsolete, mythological, folkloric contents. It is absolutely necessary that this proper claim be inscribed within a broader theoretical framework, equipped with a fully developed hierarchy of elements. Religious freedom requires in the first place the definition of a correct relationship between religions and the state. In this sense it is necessary to recognize that, as affirmed by the French historian René Rémond, "contrary to a reductive representation, the relationship between religion and society does not take place entirely in a tête-à-tête between politics and religion. The relationship is triangular: beside the state and religion, there is the society that today defines itself as civil."[73] The public expression of the religions is therefore neither undue interference nor the result of some privilege conceded by the state but is rather the consequence of their natural operation, through intermediate bodies, in a civil society in which they are full-fledged members. It is necessary, therefore, that our pluralistic societies politically institute a regime of "healthy secularism"[74] or effective "aconfessionality," in which the state does not make its own any of the cultural identities, interests, or expectations of the subjects who inhabit society but instead opens and makes equally practicable for all civil subjects the public sphere of encounter and deliberation. This consideration implies above all that religious freedom is not to be instituted by the state but rather must be recognized and promoted as inherent to the human person. In this respect the "Anglo-Saxon"—and in particular American—ideal of fundamental human rights, without denying the difficulties in which this has found itself in recent times,[75] is traditionally better equipped than the "continental" one.

A Vast Challenge

These very brief remarks demonstrate the complexity of the issue of religious freedom, but above all they highlight how, today more than ever, this represents the most sensitive litmus test of the level of civilization of our pluralistic societies.

Religious freedom in particular appears today as the encapsulation of a much broader challenge: that of the elaboration and practice, on the local and universal levels, of new anthropological, sociological, and cosmological foundations of the coexistence proper to civil societies in this third millennium. In this sense, if religious freedom—which constitutes the emblematic expression of freedom of conscience and therefore also concerns those who do not believe—does not become realized freedom, placed at the head of the scale of fundamental rights, the whole scale is destined to crumble.

No Return to the Past

Obviously, this process cannot signify a return to the past but must take place with respect for the pluralistic nature of contemporary society,[76] meaning—as I have had the opportunity to say on other occasions—in the context of the pursuit of the *practical common good of being together*,[77] within which the different identities communicate in a local dialectic of recognition and also of competition, regulated by the public authority.

6

For a Shared Journey in Pluralistic Society

I would like to refer briefly to a condition that I believe is indispensable for this arduous but pressing journey.

The teachings of *Dignitatis Humanae*, an expression of the religious freedom inaugurated by the Edict of Milan, established that adherence to the truth is possible only as a voluntary personal act and that outside coercion is contrary to its nature. It must also be recognized, however, that the realization of this twofold condition depends upon a personal commitment to the truth. In fact, to pursue "the duty, and therefore the right, to seek the truth" (*Dignitatis Humanae*, section 3) removes religious freedom from the suspicion of being another name for religious indifferentism, which presents itself as a specific worldview, at least practical, and at the current historical juncture tends to hegemonize the others.

In order to understand well the nature of this duty/right, we must reflect for a moment on the risk that the two principles recalled by *Dignitatis Humanae* might be obfuscated today.

A First Risk

First, if it is true that under today's prevailing cultural attitude the truth is considered only in relationship to the subject and his freedom—a prevalence that not rarely falls into subjectivism and the consequent relativism—it is also true that religious adherence to established traditions is too often lived in reaction and therefore is increasingly conceived of only in terms of public, community, social life, to the point that it is rather difficult to use words like "personal," "intimate," "interiority," and "singular" without a derogatory connotation. Religious (or at least Christian) culture, in short, seems sometimes to have lent to subjectivism the whole language of singularity that in reality is originally its own (Kierkegaard *docet*).

A Second Risk

The second affirmation also contains a presupposition that has become flimsy, namely that the existential quest for the truth is still indispensable today. This is no longer obvious, not only because of the well-known weakening of the idea of truth but also because human existence is no longer spontaneously thought of (as it was since the *Nichomachean Ethics*)[78] in terms of an organized system with a single end: the good life for the individual and for society.

The first preoccupation of today seems, in fact, to have become asking oneself if it makes sense, in general, to live in view of an ultimate end, or if human existence is not rather the aggregate of systems of partial meaning that cannot be compared with one another.[79] According to this vision, the very idea of seeking an ultimate and therefore religious truth simply loses its meaning.[80] And yet the experience common to every man of every time and place attests that the search for a significance and direction—in a word, for meaning—is at the heart of human experience. It blossoms in the ego's encounter with reality, not because circumstances determine case by case what is the truth but because the Truth, transcendent and absolute, is not a collection of notions but a living and personal reality that engages the universal experience of disproportion between existence and its meaning and therefore does not cease to call human freedom to account for its decision.

The Truth Is Seeking Us

What can be said, then, in response to those who do not acknowledge the obligation to seek the truth in order to adhere to it? The free invitation that is addressed to them to reflect on what makes up the duty and the right to seek the truth is decisive. Augustine, an expressive genius of human unease, grasped the secret of this: "It is not we who possess the Truth after having sought it, but it is the Truth who seeks and possesses us."[81] The truth, through the significance of relationships, circumstances, and situations of life (of which every man is the protagonist), presents itself to us as "the serious case" of human existence and human coexistence. The truth that seeks us is documented in the inextinguishable yearning with which man aspires to it: "*Quid enim fortius desiderat anima quam veritatem?*"[82] A yearning that respects the freedom of all, including of those who call themselves agnostic, indifferent, or atheist.

In my view, this is a decisive consideration in the context of present-day pluralistic societies. Only a freedom that is seeking the truth is truly capable of opening a space in which the good of communication among subjects and their mutual recognition may be effectively guaranteed. The affirmation of a truth devoid of freedom would give rise to an unceasing and ultimately violent clash of opposing worldviews, while a freedom detached from the truth would result in the very impossibility of communicating or at the most in dialogue as an end in itself.

The assertion of religious freedom would become absolutely empty if it did not presuppose human beings who personally and intimately cannot renounce the desire to adhere to an ultimate truth that determines their lives.

A Future of Peace for Pluralistic Societies

Here a terrain opens on which cultural (and educational) effort should be a priority in our Western societies, where the proliferation of superficial freedoms seems to be accompanied by an increasing restriction of profound inner freedom.

Understood in this way, a comprehensive conception of religious freedom has important social and political implications. On the one hand it limits the claim that the sociopolitical dimension should become the horizon of the human person, while on the other it suggests the enhancement of a protagonism, typical of civil society, that no democratic state can do without. The narration, in view of reciprocal public recognition, of *free religious subjects bearing "substantive" ethics* appears to be indispensable. It seems to me the path to a future of peace for our pluralistic societies.

This is the terrain on which it is truly decided what is the use of freedom understood as the absence of coercion, where it could lead, and for what it should be expended.

The Good of the Communication and Aconfessionality of the State

Religious freedom, I insist, signals that the sociopolitical dimension cannot be the horizon of the human person[83] and emphasizes a protagonism, typical of civil society, that no democratic state can do without.

In my view, these are two coordinates that constitute an essential point of reference for any hypothesis of a humanly sustainable good life.[84]

Pluralistic Contemporary Society

Nonetheless, if the Christian "claim" is also that of safeguarding the authentic meaning of freedom and more generally of being able to offer valuable guidance for life in society, it is evident that this discussion cannot be conducted without addressing the contemporary situation of unprecedented *plurality* in which we find ourselves speaking and acting. This is absolutely not a matter of proposing a nostalgic return to the past, which, as we have seen, has not been faithful to the truth of religious freedom.

If pluralism represents a problem today, this is in part because of the crisis of the communicative relationship into which Western societies are plunged. The end of modernity and of its great narratives has involved, among other things, an incapacity to elaborate a universal code of understanding. In the absence of this code, it is natural that the coexistence of different and contrasting conceptions of the world should seem ever more impracticable.

The Principle of Communication

The difficulty in communicating is a symptom that we cannot underestimate, if we want to defend the public sphere of democratic coexistence. Jürgen Habermas has always been particularly attentive to this indicator: "The condition in which a democracy finds itself can be accepted only by taking the pulse of its political public sphere."[85]

In order to configure correctly the relationships among the various personal and community subjects in a pluralistic society, including the religious subjects, one must therefore start from the *principle of communication*, to be understood, in the strongest sense, as a fundamental "holding in common" and "being in common" (which for Christians is a reflection of the most radical and originating communication, that among the Persons of the Most Holy Trinity).[86]

Precisely because of its profound nature, this communication can never be taken for granted but must be considered the result of a decision, implicit as this may be. One can therefore certainly speak about a good of communication that also represents the primary political reality. In effect, and in spite of the abundance of voices to the contrary, life in society needs in any case an idea of goodness in which all can recognize themselves. As the French philosopher Jacques Maritain understood, in a pluralistic context such an idea cannot be gathered from a shared theoretical conception of the world[87] but coincides with the undeniable and fundamental good of *being in common* itself or, if one prefers, the practical good of being together. This concept, as is well known, was central in the social magisterium of John Paul II, who always insisted on the primary good constituted by this being together.[88]

A Practical Common Thought

This communicative foundation, which could appear flimsy, in reality requires indispensable and demanding conditions. Communicating, in fact, requires recognizing the other as a full-fledged interlocutor, without discrimination, with justice, so that politics may truly be the domain in which the "many" may contribute responsibly to the common good. This is why the presumed neutrality of political conceptions and decisions that exclude every religious reference from the public sphere is not convincing: the result of this orientation, in fact, is not common practical thought but rather a lowest common denominator with respect to which cultural differences undergo an estranging privatization.[89] The truly public and therefore authentically aconfessional is only the space that wagers upon the freedom of citizens, believers and nonbelievers, and makes it possible to "recount oneself," which means undertaking the work of expressing the meaning of one's own experience, according to a logic—as Ricoeur teaches—of reciprocal, albeit laborious, recognition.[90] It is clear that in this reciprocal narration the different subjects will be able and moreover will be invited to draw from time to time upon the traditions to which they belong, whether these be religious or secular, enriching the primary practical consensus with additional elements. This requires abandoning purely oppositional and mistakenly "neutralist" significances of secularism: if the objective of politics is common practical thought, believing citizens as well must be able to have their say, naturally on the conditions of not turning politics into ethics or religion and of engaging in their social activism.

The Responsibility of "Translation"

This political conception has as an important corollary the responsibility of the *translation* of one's own vision of the world into a language that is understandable even to those who do not share it, a task that does not fall only to believing citizens but must be understood—as Habermas correctly recalls—as "a [common] collaborative effort."[91] Moreover, this seems to be the position that, beginning in the middle of the 1980s, the American Supreme Court took when, attenuating the previous rigidly separationist logic, it made its own the constitutional principle that affirms and promotes the equal treatment of believers and nonbelievers.[92]

7

The Public Engagement
of Catholics

If it is true that it is a duty of the state to guarantee space for the public expression of religion and for communication among subjects, it is likewise true that the quality of its contents will depend on the vitality of those who inhabit it. In this sense, the civil and political engagement of Christians is particularly urgent, as Benedict XVI does not cease to recall. This is a matter not only of defending a particular position and conception of life from external attacks but also of incorporating into the public debate reasons that are potentially valid for all.

The "Duty" of Testimony

This naturally does not imply that the proposal of Catholics, in order to be advanced publicly with full legitimacy, must be in harmony with the views prevalent in society. Many questions that, at least in the West, touch on the issue of religious freedom today refer in reality to the very vision of the human and to the relative "conflict of interpretations": "The point, then, is that, if we fail to understand that the present crisis is at root one regarding the nature of the human being, our political strategies, however effective in the short term, will over the long term serve to strengthen the very assumptions that have generated the crisis in the first place. This does not mean that strategies that speak of rights in the liberal idiom cannot be justified for prudential reasons—even for a prudence that is Gospel-inspired. It means simply that even these strategies must be integrated as far as possible, from the beginning, into a more adequate sense of rights based on a fuller vision of the human person. . . ."[93]

What is at stake, therefore, is the opportunity for Christians and more generally for believers not only to express themselves publicly but in doing so to render adequate reason for their experience, which moves the emphasis from the right of believers to their duty of testimony.

Christianity, in fact, claims to respond to the expectations and needs of the whole man and of all men, as a proposal and never as an imposition. Habermas maintains in this regard as entirely justifiable, beyond the effort of translating proposals into an accredited public language, also "the admission of untranslated religious statements into the public sphere." The reason is simple: a truly democratic state "cannot discourage believers and religious communities from expressing themselves as such politically as well, because it cannot know if, in the contrary case, secular society would not be deprived of important resources of creation of meaning."[94]

No Hegemony

It could be added that any amputated or partial interpretation of Christianity, favoring some aspects to the detriment of others, would inevitably end up being exploited, undermining the very originality of the Christian proposal, and reducing Catholics to irrelevance. It is also worthwhile to recall what the

Second Vatican Council teaches with regard to the role of the lay faithful in society: "It is their special task to order and to throw light upon these affairs in such a way that they may come into being and then continually increase according to Christ to the praise of the Creator and the Redeemer."[95] This is not an invitation to pursue hegemony but rather recognition of the fact that a faith lived out completely has an indispensable anthropological, social, and cosmological relevance, full of rather concrete political consequences.[96] If one bears witness in every area of human existence, including that of politics and party, to one's own convictions, this does not injure anyone's rights. On the contrary, while these are promoted, one sets in motion the virtuous search for noble "compromise" (*cum promitto*) on specific goods of an ethical, social, cultural, economic, and political character.

If agreement on indispensable principles should not be possible with the other "inhabitants" of pluralist society, recourse can be made to conscientious objection. Contrary to what some maintain, conscientious objection has not only the private purpose of exempting the subject from behaviors that are unacceptable to him but also that of calling to general attention issues for which an adequate sensitivity is not believed to have been formed yet, thus contributing in a valuable way to the public debate.[97] This social dimension of conscientious objection requires more than ever an in-depth reflection that unfortunately is still lacking today.

The "Price" of Testimony

We are aware that today this option is in danger of not being adequately guaranteed by the law and therefore of involving a personal price. It therefore situates the Christian within the logic of testimony, which, as Benedict XVI recalled on the occasion of the recent Synod of Bishops on the new evangelization for the transmission of the Christian faith, is always a "confession" and therefore "brings with it the martyrological element." Testimony is not, the pope notes, "only something of the heart and of the mouth, but also of the mind; it has to be thought about and thus, thought of and intelligently conceived, it touches the other person."[98]

This task is a demanding one, but it is also fascinating.

Notes

1. See L. Pietri and J. Flamant, "La crisi dell'Impero romano e l'affermazione di una nuova religiosità," in *Storia del Cristianesimo: Religione, Politica, Cultura*, vol. 2, ed. G. Alberigo (Rome: Borla and Città nuova, 2000), 25–52; J. Zeiler, "Le grandi persecuzioni della metà del III secolo e il periodo di pace religiosa dal 260 al 302," in *Storia della Chiesa*, vol. 2, ed. A. Fliche and V. Martin (Cinisello Balsamo, Italy: San Paolo, 1995), 225–46.

2. See F. Kolb, "L'ideologia tetrarchica e la politica religiosa di Diocleziano," in *I Cristiani e l'Impero nel IV secolo: Colloquio sul Cristianesimo nel mondo antico*, ed. G. Bonamente and A. Nestori (Macerata, Italy: Università degli Studi di macerate and Pubblicazioni della Facoltà di Lettere e Filosofia, 1988), 17–44.

3. See L. Pieri, "Le resistenze: dalla polemica pagana alla persecuzione di Diocleziano," in Alberigo, *Storia del Cristianesimo*, vol. 2, 156–83; J. Zeiler, "L'ultima

persecuzione," in Fliche and Martin, *Storia della Chiesa*, vol. 2, 633–63.

4. For a description and evaluation of the anti-Christian edicts of Diocletian and Maximian, see P. Siniscalco, *Il cammino di Cristo nell'Impero romano* (Bari, Italy: Laterza 2009), 61–77 and 92–96.

5. "The general persecutions undoubtedly put the Christian communities to a hard test. Taking into account the nature of the sources available to us, it is impossible to establish an exact balance in numeric terms: the regions and circumstances were different, and the total number of victims—those who paid with their lives or remained mutilated after torture—cannot be calculated," Pietri, "Le resistenze," 182. See also M. Sordi, *I cristiani e l'Impero romano* (Milan: Jaca Book, 2004), 167–68.

6. On the failure of the tetrarchic construction of Diocletian, see S. Mazzarino, *L'Impero romano* (Bari, Italy: Laterza, 1993), 593–99.

7. The text of the edict of Galerius is preserved in Lactantius, *De mortibus persecutorum*, 34; Eusebius of Caesarea, *Historia Ecclesiastica* vol. 8, 17, 6 10. The Italian text can be found in Eusebius of Caesarea, *Storia Ecclesiastica* vol. 2, Collana di testi Patristici 159, (Rome: Città nuova, 2001), 180–81.

8. See Siniscalco, *Il cammino di Cristo*, 163.

9. See J. R. Palanque, "L'impero cristiano," in Fliche and Martin, *Storia della Chiesa*, vol. 3/1, 17 83; C. Pietri, "La conversione: Propaganda e realtà della legge e dell'evergetismo," in Alberigo, *Storia del Cristianesimo: Religione, Politica, Cultura*, vol. 2, 187–223.

10. On this topic see F. Braschi, "La 'conversione' di Costantino: Riflessioni a partire dai criteri di lettura delle fonti antiche," *La Scuola Cattolica* 135 (2007): 115–49.

11. G. Lombardi, *Persecuzioni, laicità, libertà religiosa: Dall'Editto di Milano alla "Dignitatis humanae"* (Rome: Studium, 1991), 128.

12. Ibid., 124–25.

13. See Lactantius, *De mortibus persecutorum*, 48. The translation of the text from the original Latin of Lactantius is from L. Martinez Ferrer and P. L. Guiducci (eds.), *Fontes: Documenti fondamentali di storia della Chiesa* (Cinisello Balsamo, Italy: San Paolo, 2005), 70–73.

14. Eusebius of Caesarea, *Historia Ecclesiastica*, vol. 10, 5, 2–14. This English translation is from newadvent.org.

15. For a comprehensive evaluation of the Edict of Milan, see Sordi, *I cristiani e l'Impero Romano*, 171–83, and Siniscalco, *Il cammino di Cristo*, 163–67. See also P. Veyne, *Quando l'Europa è diventata Cristiana (312–394): Costantino, la conversione, l'Impero* (Milan: Garzanti, 2010).

16. Eusebius of Caesarea, *Ecclesiastical History* vol. 10, I, 8; 2, I, in Eusebius of Caesarea, *Storia Ecclesiastica/2*, 215. Considering the Edict of Milan as an antecedent of religious freedom in the modern sense does not mean misunderstanding the fact that "the fragility of this ideal balance did not delay in manifesting itself and was broken with the rupture of the balance of forces between Constantine and Licinius, with the former considering the agreement of Milan the minimal request and the latter the maximum concession in the matter of religious legislation" (Sordi, *I cristiani e l'Impero Romano*, 182). This fragility, in real terms, led to the intermingling of political power and religion, generically identified with the term "Constantinianism" and definitively shelved with the conciliar declaration *Dignitatis Humanae.*

17. Cf. Lombardi, *Persecuzioni, laicità, libertà religiosa*, 18–19 and 136.

18. Cf. G. del Pozo Abejón, *La Iglesia y la libertad religiosa* (Madrid: BAC, 2007); Lombardi, *Persecuzioni, laicità, libertà religiosa*, 9-30; N. Lobkowicz, "Il Faraone Amenhotep e la Dignitatis Humanae," *Oasis* 8 (2008): 17–23.

19. Cf. P. Frezza, "L'esperienza della tolleranza religiosa fra pagani e cristiani dal IV al V sec. nell'oriente ellenistico," *Studia et Documenta Historiae et Iuris* 55 (1989): 41–97.

20. Cf. P. De Labriolle, "L'imperatore Giuliano," in Fliche and Martin, *Storia della Chiesa* vol. 3/1, 227–36; J. Fla-

mant and C. Pietri, "La dissoluzione del sistema costantiniano: Giuliano l'Apostata (361–363)," in Alberigo, *Storia del Cristianesimo*, vol. 2, 325–40; Lombardi, *Persecuzioni, laicità, libertà religiosa*, 140–46.

21. Cf. C. Pietri, "Il fallimento dell'unità 'imperiale' in Africa: La resistenza donatista (to 361)," in Alberigo, *Storia del Cristianesimo*, vol. 2, 224–42.

22. Cf. C. Pietri, "I successi: La soppressione del paganesimo e il trionfo del cattolicesimo di stato," in Alberigo, *Storia del Cristianesimo*, vol. 2, 381–413; G. Bardy and J. R. Palanque, "Graziano e Teodosio: La nuova politica ecclesiastica," in Fliche and Martin, *Storia della Chiesa*, vol. 3/1, 353–61.

23. Well known in this regard is the conflict with the emperor Theodosius regarding the massacre of the innocent and unarmed in the "massacre of Thessalonica," a vendetta, approved by the emperor himself, for the killing of a military commandant. Cf. G. Vismara, "Ambrogio e Teodosio: I limiti del potere," *Studia et Documenta historiae et Iuris* 56 (1990): 256–69; G. Vismara, "Ambrogio: Un vescovo per una città," *Ambrosius* 62, no. 2 (1986): 129–40; D. Lassandro, "Ambrogio, Teodosio e il perdono," in *Responsabilità, perdono e vendetta nel mondo antico*, ed. M. Sordi (Milan: Vita e Pensiero, 1998), 291–301.

24. Cf. C. Pasini, *Ambrogio di Milano* (Cinisello Balsamo, Italy: San Paolo, 1996), 103–17.

25. Augustine, Letter 93, chap. 5, para. 17. This English translation is from newadvent.org.

26. Jerome, *Vita S. Malachi* I.

27. Lombardi, *Persecuzioni, laicità, libertà religiosa,* 148.

28. Lobkowicz, "Il Faraone Amenhotep e la Dignitatis Humanae," 19.

29. Thomas Aquinas, *Summa Theologiae* IIa IIae, q. 10, a. 8 co. See also Thomas Aquinas, *Summa Theologiae* IIa IIae, q. 11, a. 3.

30. Lombardi, *Persecuzioni, laicità, libertà religiosa,* 21.

31. Cf. S. Cavalotto, "La guerra dei Trent'anni e il consolidamento delle confessioni fino alla pace di Westfalia," in Fliche and Martin, *Storia della Chiesa,* vol. 18/2, ed. L. Mezzadri (Cinisello Balsamo, Italy: San Paolo, 1988), 171–220.

32. Cf. Lombardi, *Persecuzioni, laicità, libertà religiosa,* 23–24.

33. Cf. J. Locke, *Lettera sulla tolleranza,* ed. C. A. Viano (Bari, Italy: Laterza, 1994).

34. Cf. C. Anderson, "Religione e politica nello spirito americano," *Oasis* 2 (2005): 94–96.

35. I follow the presentation of the argument made by Gerardo del Pozo Abejón in *La Iglesia y la libertad religiosa*, 77–139.

36. "The French Revolution of 1789, under the impulse of the ideas of the Enlightenment, soon gave voice to the secularizing tendencies present among some of its supporters. The requirement of separation between state and Church, maintained to be distinctive of the new order, also had its roots in anti-clerical and irreligious motivations that, mainly spread among parts of the middle class and intellectual circles, stood in opposition to Christian thought, which was believed to have been superseded by the new philosophical currents and by the achievements of scientific discovery. This was not a matter only of sanctioning the emancipation of reason from every form of external dependence, and therefore of rejecting the authority of religious dogmas and traditional churches, but also proposing a new secularist creed, a secular religion, which amounts to saying 'a sort of real and proper religion without clergy, without dogma, and without ritual. A completely secular religion, which exalted values like progress, science, the defense of human rights, and the assertion of the absolute autonomy of reason.'" M. Margotti, *Religioni e secolarizzazioni: Ebraismo, cristianesimo e Islam nel mondo globale* (Torino, Italy: Rosenberg & Sellier, 2012), 92–93.

37. del Pozo Abejón, *La Iglesia y la libertad religiosa*, 133.

38. Cf. B. Valuet, *Le droit à la liberté religieuse dans la Tradition de l'Église* (Le Barroux, France: Éditions Sainte Madeleine, 2005).

39. Cf. del Pozo Abejón, *La Iglesia y la libertad religiosa*, 141–78.

40. Ibid., 155.

41. On the process of drafting the declaration *Dignitatis Humanae*, cf.: J. Hamer and Y. Congar, "La liberté religieuse: Déclaration 'Dignitatis humanae personae,'" vol. 60 of *Unam Sanctam* (Paris: Editions du Cerf, 1967); S. Scatena, *La fatica della libertà: L'elaborazione della dichiarazione "Dignitatis humanae" sulla libertà religiosa del Vaticano II* (Bologna, Italy: Il Mulino, 2003).

42. Cf. A. Scola, "Un'adeguata ermeneutica conciliare," *Il regno Documenti* 17 (2012), 538–49.

43. According to del Pozo Abejón, there are two essential innovations in the declaration: "The first and principal innovation: the declaration that every man has the right to religious freedom.... The second innovation is the explanation of the essential almonds of freedom just cleared. In it are described the active subject (the human person) and the passive (individual persons, groups, and political power), the foundation (dignity of the human person), the nature (natural/fundamental law that must be recognized civilly), the object (immunity from external coercion in order to act socially according to

conscience in religious matters) and the limits on the extent of the object (within the due limits, the just public order)," del Pozo Abejón, *La Iglesia y la libertad religiosa,* 209–10.

44. Ibid., 219.

45. Even if some council fathers from communist regimes asked that reference not be made to this limitation because it could justify abuses on the part of the state, the final text included it because it was consistent with the traditional doctrine of common good. In this regard it is useful to consult the contributions of council father Karol Wojtyla on religious freedom. Cf. G. Richi Alberti, *Karol Wojtyla, uno stile conciliare* (Venice: Marcianum Press, 2012), 175–235.

46. Lobkowicz, "Il Faraone Amenhotep e la Dignitatis Humanae," 18.

47. Del Pozo Abejón, *La Iglesia y la libertad religiosa,* 264–65. This description of the conciliar teaching harmonizes with the one by Pietro Pavan in an article that has become a classic on the subject: P. Pavan, "Il diritto della libertà religiosa nella dichiarazione conciliare 'Dignitatis humanae,'" *Concilium* 2, no. 5 (1966): 31–46.

48. John Paul II, "Message on the value and content of freedom of conscience and of religion," November 14, 1980. Cf. F. D'Agostino, *Jus quia Justum: Lezioni di filosofia del diritto e della religione* (Torino, Italy, Giappichelli, 2012), 111.

49. Ibid., 113.

50. Cf. John Paul II, *Veritatis Splendor,* 54. Cf. also A. Scola, "La prospettiva teologica di Veritatis splendor," in L. Melina and J. Noriega, *Camminare nella luce: Prospettive della teologia morale a partire da Veritatis splendor* (Rome: Lateran University Press, 2004), 65–81.

51. Proof of this is the fruitful magisterium in this regard of Blessed John Paul II. Cf. A. Colombo, ed. *La libertà religiosa negli insegnamenti di Giovanni Paolo II (1978–1998)* (Milan: Vita e Pensiero, 2000).

52. Cf. Benedict XVI, "Ad Romanam Curiam ob omina natalicia: Die 22 decembris 2005," *Acta Apostolicae Sedis* 98 (2006), 40–53 (quoted material at 50–51).

53. It is useful to read, both for its theoretical reflections and for information relative to the different situations, the volume of the proceedings of the plenary assembly of the Pontifical Academy of Social Sciences of April 29–May 3, 2011: Pontifical Academy of Social Sciences Acta 17, *Universal Rights in a World of Diversity: The Case of Religious Freedom,* ed. M. A. Glendon and H. F. Zacher (Vatican City: Libreria Editrice Vaticana, 2012). In particular see the contributions of R. Minnerath, F. R. Hittinger, O. Höffe, A. D. Hertzke, A. A. Anna'im, R. Buttiglione, J. Martínez Torrón, W. Cole Durham Jr., M. Cartabia, and J.H.H. Weiler. Cf. also

J. Rodriguez, *Secolarismo e libertà religiosa: Atti del Congresso Internazionale nel trentesimo anniversario della promulgazione della dichiarazione conciliare Dignitatis humanae, Roma 5–7 dicembre 1995* (Vatican City: Libreria Editrice Vaticana, 1998).

54. Cf. B. J. Grim and R. Finke, *The Price of Freedom Denied: Religious Persecution and Conflict in the Twenty-first Century* (New York: Cambridge University Press, 2011). See also this 2012 report published by the Pew Research Center: Pew Research Religion & Public Life Forum, "Rising Tide of Restrictions on Religion," September 20, 2012, www.pewforum.org/2012/09/20/rising-tide-of-restrictions-on-religion-findings/.

55. In its regularly published reports, Aid to the Church in Need has made important contributions to an understanding of the situation in which religious freedom finds itself all over the world, country by country. See in particular: Aiuto alla Chiesa che Soffre, *Rapporto 2012: Libertà religiosa nel mondo* (Rome: Aiuto alla Chiesa che Soffre, 2012).

56. Cf. O. Roy, "The Transformation of the Arab World," *Journal of Democracy* 23, no. 3 (July 2012): 5–18.

57. For the voices that tend in this direction, see M. Marzouki, "La libertà di coscienza, principio di ogni cittadinanza," *Oasis* 16 (2012): 12–13; Y. Ben Achour, "La misura della libertà: libertà senza misura?" *Oasis* 16 (2012): 15–18.

58. Aiuto alla Chiesa che Soffre, 101–30, quoted material at 101.

59. Observatory on Intolerance and Discrimination against Christians in Europe, Report 2011 (Vienna: Observatory on Intolerance and Discrimination against Christians in Europe, 2012), 9, available at www.intolerance againstchristians.eu/fileadmin/user_upload/ Report_2011_on_Intolerance_and_Discrimination _against_Christians_in_Europe_Webversion.pdf.

60. Administrative Committee of the United States Conference of Catholic Bishops, "United for Religious Freedom," March 14, 2012, www.usccb .org/issues-and-action/religious-liberty/march-14 -statement-on-religious-freedom-and-hhs-mandate .cfm; United States Conference of Catholic Bishops, Ad Hoc Committee for Religious Liberty, "Our First, Most Cherished Liberty: A Statement on Religious Liberty," March 2012, www.usccb.org/issues -and-action/religious-liberty/our-first-most-cherished -liberty.cfm.

61. This element would decisively alter the balance presented by *Dignitatis Humanae,* sections 3–4.

62. Curiously, the term "conversion" is completely absent from the text of the conciliar declaration, where the verb "convert" appears only once (in section 11) in a reference to the work of the apostles.

63. Cf. K. N. Hylton, Y. Rodionova, and F. Deng, "Church and State: An Economic Analysis," *American Law and Economics Review* 13, no. 2 (2011): 402–52.

64. Cf. E. Böckenförde, "Die Entstehung des Staates als Vorgang der Säkularisation" (1967), in ibid., in *Recht, Staat, Freiheit* (Frankfurt, Germany: Suhrkamp, 1991), 92–114.

65. Cf. M. J. Sandel, *Giustizia: Il nostro bene comune* (Milan: Feltri nelli, 2012), especially 275–301.

66. R. Rorty, "La priorità della democrazia sulla filosofia," in *Scritti filosofici*, vol. I, Italian translation ed. A. G. Gargani (Rome and Bari, Italy: Laterza, 1994), 248.

67. Cf. Benedict XVI, speech at the Basilica of the Immaculate Conception, April 16, 2008.

68. Cf. C. Durham, "Perspectives on Religious Liberty: a Comparative Framework," in J. D. van der Vyver and J. Witte (eds.), *Religious Human Rights in Global Perspective* (The Hague and Boston: Springer, 1996), 24ff.

69. "The problem, in fact, would receive a new configuration if the public authorities were truly conceived of and practiced as custodians and administrators of a common good, meaning a community of national life in which all the cultural traditions and religious identities play an active part. In a definitive sense the problem is the kind

of relationships that the public authorities maintain with civil society, understood as a pluralistic relational fabric, the significance of which should be emphasized as much as possible rather than being controlled. This has its concrete verification to the extent to which the institutional orientations and public policies effectively favor forms of solidarity and subsidiarity, because it is here that the impartiality of the rules that apply to all and the greatest possible pluralism of identities come together." F. Botturi, "La politica favorisca il maggior pluralismo possibile delle identità," *Avvenire Milano Sette*, December 16, 2012, I. See also A. Scola, *Una nuova laicità: Temi per una società plurale* (Venice: Marsilio, 2007), 104–5.

70. Worthy of particular attention for its clarity and paradigmatic value is ruling number 203 of 1989 of the Constitutional Court. In it, section 4 states: "The values recalled contribute, along with others (articles 7, 8, and 20 of the Constitution), to structuring the supreme principle of the secularism of the state, which is one of the features of the form of state delineated in the Constitutional Charter of the Republic. The principle of secularism, as it emerges from articles 2, 3, 7, 8, 19, and 20 of the Constitution, implies not the indifference of the state with respect to religion, but a guarantee of the state for the safeguarding of freedom of religion, in a framework of confessional and cultural pluralism."

71. "It is true that for Italian constitutional doctrine the secularism of the state is interpreted as collaborative secularism with the religious realities recognized as being present in the country. But this coexists with the recurrent denunciation of interference with and aggression against the secularism of the state with regard to the legislative orientations that, although they are subjected to the voting and the rules of the majority, come from political sectors inspired by a religious conception; or with the denunciation of violation of secularism apart from public support for initiatives of public utility, like the non-state schools. Positions that bear witness that the public square is still conceived of as such in the sense of being religiously neutral." Botturi, "La politica favorisca il maggior pluralismo possibile," I.

72. A. Scola, *Buone ragioni per la vita in comune* (Milan: Mondadori, 2010), 16–17.

73. R. Rémond, Religion et Société en Europe: La sécularisation aux XIXe et XXe siècles: 1789–2000 (Paris: Seuil, 2001), 13.

74. An expression coined by Pius XII and frequently recalled by Benedict XVI.

75. In the United States the past half century has seen the catastrophic collapse of traditional Protestant communities (Methodist, Presbyterian, Lutheran, Episcopalian,

etc.). At the strictly numerical level, these have been partially replaced by the new independent communities (Evangelicals, Mormons), but these latter have demonstrated themselves to be completely sterile culturally and incapable of upholding a unified national culture such as there was until around the end of the 1960s. See R. Douthat, *Bad Religion: How We Became a Nation of Heretics* (New York: Free Press, 2012).

76. See A. Scola, *Una nuova laicità. Temi per una società plurale,* Marsilio, Venice, 2007.

77. See A. Scola, "La società plural: Prospettiva teologica," in G. Richi Alberti (ed.), *Pensare la società plurale* (Venice: Marcianum Press, 2010), 7–22.

78. Cf. Sandel, *Giustizia,* 207–33.

79. "There is a third possibility, meaning that in modern society, in the face of the plurality of religious options, or, more modestly, overcome by the dream of material happiness, there is an abrupt disappearance of the reference to the transcendent, to its values and its traditions in the forms known until now, making irrelevant in the horizon of the individual life the reference to a 'completely different' dimension." Margotti, 152.

80. "The strongest theories, nonetheless, always have to do with religion. And this is the way it should be, because ultimately every human culture is religious, defined by

what its members believe with regard to whatever matter is in question and from this what that matter demands from them. And that matter does not necessarily have to be a personified God: they can be the iron laws of Marxism, the cult of blood and territory, the hypothesis of Gaia, the church of the free market, the cult of the imperial self. As Bob Dylan said in one of his songs, 'you're gonna have to serve somebody,' and every culture does." Douthat, *Bad Religion*, 2 (our translation).

81. This is how Benedict XVI describes "the experience of Augustine." Benedict XVI, General Audience, Rome, November 14, 2012.

82. Augustine, *Tractates on the Gospel of Saint John*, 26.5: "What can man desire more powerfully than the truth?"

83. Cf. John Paul II, Address to members of the diplomatic corps accredited to the Holy See, January 9, 1989.

84. A. Scola, "La solidarietà, esigenza etica e speranza spirituale?" in *La rivista del Clero Italiano* 93, no. 3 (2012): 168–82.

85. J. Habermas, *La condizione intersoggettiva*, trans. M. Carpitella (Rome and Bari, Italy: Laterza, 2005), 18.

86. The idea of the obsolescence of liberal political "neutrality" and proceduralism in terms of "common life" (Charles Larmore), "shared common good" (Charles

Taylor), and justice, good life, and the common good
(Michael Sandel) is significantly present in these authors of liberal origin but sensitive to the demands of
communitarianism; the idea of political life as founded
on the communicative relationship is fundamental for
Karl-Otto Apel and Jürgen Habermas and in general
for authors of discursive ethics. The observations of
Romano Guardini are illuminating: R. Guardini, "Il
significato del dogma del Dio trinitario per la vita etica
della comunità," in *Opera omnia VI: Scritti politici* (Brescia,
Italy: Morcelliana, 2005), 97.

87. J. Maritain, "La personne et le bien commun," in *Oeuvres
complètes*, vol. 9: 1947–1951 (Fribourg, Switzerland, and
Paris: Éditions Universitaires and Éditions Saint Paul,
1990), 167–237, referenced material at 178.

88. One important reference is the Letter to Families of
1994, in particular at number 15: "In the first place,
the family achieves the good of 'being together.' This
is the good par excellence of marriage (hence its indis-
solubility) and of the family community. It could also
be defined as a good of the subject as such. Just as the
person is a subject, so too is the family, since it is made
up of persons, who, joined together by a profound bond
of communion, form a single communal subject. Indeed, the family is more a subject than any other social
institution: more so than the nation or the State, more
so than society and international organizations. These
societies, especially nations, possess a proper subjectiv-

ity to the extent that they receive it from persons and their families."

89. Cf. F. Botturi, "Secolarizzazione e laicità," in P. Donati (ed.), *Laicità: la ricerca dell'universale nelle differenze* (Bologna, Italy: Il Mulino, 2008), 295–337. Cf. also M. Gauchet, *La religion dans la démocratie: Parcours de la laïcité* (Paris: Gallimard, 1998); M. Troper, French Secularism or Laicité, *Cardozo Law Review* 21 (2000), 1267–84.

90. P. Ricoeur, *Parcours de la reconnaissance* (Paris: Editions Stock, 2004). Alasdair MacIntyre, Charles Taylor, and more recently Seyla Benhabib have extensively developed the theme of dialogical communication.

91. J. Habermas, *Tra scienza e fede* (Rome and Bari, Italy: Laterza, 2006), 35.

92. Cf. J. Witte Jr. and J. Latterell, "Al di là del muro di separazione tra Chiesa e Stato," *Oasis* 14 (2011): 73–78.

93. D. L. Schindler, "The Repressive Logic of Liberal Rights: Religious Freedom, Contraceptives and the 'Phony' Argument of the *New York Times*," in *Communio* 38 (winter 2011): 523–547, quoted material at 524.

94. Habermas, *Tra scienza e fede*, 34.

95. Pope Paul VI, *Lumen Gentium*, November 21, 1964, 31.

96. On this argument I permit myself to refer to A. Scola, *La dottrina sociale della Chiesa: risorsa per una società plurale* (Milan: Vita e Pensiero, 2007).

97. Cf. D'Agostino, *Jus quia Justum*, 96.

98. Benedict XVI, "Meditation During the First General Congregation," Thirteenth Ordinary General Assembly of the Synod of Bishops, October 8, 2012.